JUV   The Blues.
ML
3521
.S45
1994

$15.95

1 2/02

On the cover A trio of legendary bluesmen—(left to right) Little Bill Gaither, Memphis Slim, and Big Bill Broonzy—perform in a Chicago club in the 1940s.

Chelsea House Publishers

Editorial Director   Richard Rennert

Executive Managing Editor   Karyn Gullen Browne

Executive Editor   Sean Dolan

Copy Chief   Robin James

Picture Editor   Adrian G. Allen

Art Director   Robert Mitchell

Manufacturing Director   Gerald Levine

Production Coordinator   Marie Claire Cebrián-Ume

Staff for The Blues

Text Editor   Marian W. Taylor

Picture Researcher   Alan Gottlieb

Book Layout   Jesse Cohen, John Infantino

First Printing

1   3   5   7   9   8   6   4   2

Library of Congress Cataloging-in-Publication Data

The Blues/[compiled by] Jerry Silverman.
1 score. — (Traditional Black Music)
Summary: A songbook of blues music with songs and captioned pictures.
  0-7910-1830-X   0-7910-1846-6 (pbk.)
1. Blues (Music)—Juvenile. [1. Blues (Music) 2. Songs.] I. Silverman, Jerry. II. Series.
M1630.18.B6256 1993   93-10213
                                                CIP ACM

PICTURE CREDITS

Bettmann: pp. 7, 13, 19, 23, 29, 35, 43, 61, 63; Frank Driggs Collection: cover; Library of Congress: pp. 32, 51, 57.

CONTENTS

Author's Preface

From ancient tribal rhythms to medieval plainsong to modern jazz, music has always had the power to touch people. And perhaps no musical form exerts a more universal appeal than the black American music called *the blues*. Every blues is the personal, creative statement of the individual who voices it, but it focuses on collective human experience: the grief and despair of lost love and lost hope. Differences—in race, gender, status, age, or language—raise barriers; common pain—expressed by the blues—transcends them all.

The blues is a direct reaction to life itself. Its style, therefore, reflects the time and place where it is voiced. The city woman who has lost her man to a glamorous competitor will complain in one set of terms; the drought-haunted farmer of the Great Depression will express his loss in another; a convict with nothing ahead of him but harsh, lonely years, in still another. But whether they are white or black, live in easy times or hard, dwell in city or country, inhabit cabins or castles, people feel the same pain: their lovers leave, their fortunes fade, their hopes dim, their hearts break. Everyone can understand and sympathize with the blues.

Out of poverty and oppression, out of broken homes and chain gangs, out of city slums and tenant farms came the black blues shouter, the street singer, the itinerant guitar picker. The burden of his (and later, her) song was humanity itself—constantly changing, seeking, despairing, and hoping:

I'm a stranger here, just blowed in your town,
I'm a stranger here, just blowed in your town,
Just because I'm a stranger everybody wants to dog me 'round.

Only one who actually sings the blues can arrive at its true definition. And to be true to the spirit of the blues, an individual must sing these songs as the spirit dictates. A real blues performance is a spontaneous act, never performed the same way twice. The blues singer reinvents the blues each time he or she sings.

Good morning, blues; blues, how do you do?
Good morning, blues; blues, how do you do?
I'm doin' all right; good mornin', how are you?

The blues, one of black America's great gifts to the nation, is also one of America's greatest contributions to world culture.

Jerry Silverman

The Contribution of Blacks to American Art and Culture

Kenneth B. Clark

Historical and contemporary social inequalities have obscured the major contribution of American blacks to American culture. The historical reality of slavery and the combined racial isolation, segregation, and sustained educational inferiority have had deleterious effects. As related pervasive social problems determine and influence the art that any group can not only experience, but also, ironically, the extent to which they can eventually contribute to the society as a whole, this tenet is even more visible when assessing the contributions made by African Americans.

All aspects of the arts have been pursued by black Americans, but music provides a special insight into the persistent and inescapable social forces to which black Americans have been subjected. One can speculate that in their preslavery patterns of life in Africa, blacks used rhythm, melody, and lyrics to hold on to reality, hope, and the acceptance of life. Later, in America, music helped blacks endure the cruelties of slavery. Spirituals and gospel music provided a medium for both communion and communication. As the black experience in America became more complex, so too did black music, which has grown and ramified, dramatically affecting the development of American music in general. The result is that today, more than ever before, black music provides a powerful lens through which we may view the history of black Americans in a new and revealing way.

"Poor Joe" Williams cuts a blues record in the 1930s. Rediscovered by blues scholars, Williams would begin a second recording career in 1958.

Appointed by his brother, Governor Pete Turney, Joe Turney became a Tennessee "long-chain man" in 1893. His job consisted of rounding up convicted prisoners in Memphis, chaining them together, and transporting them 200 miles to the state penitentiary in Nashville. As often happens in folk history, names have changed over the years; yesterday's Joe Turney is today's Joe Turner. Sometimes called the "Granddaddy of the Blues," this is one of the earliest recorded three-line blues.

JOE TURNER

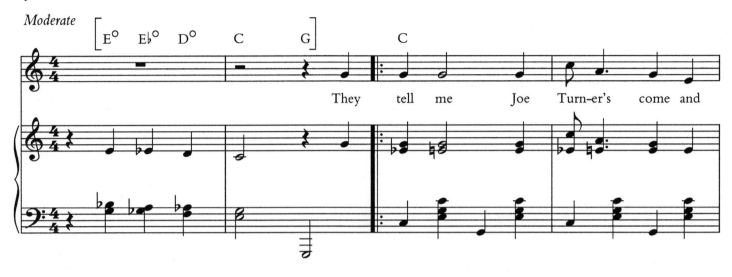

He come with forty links of chain.
He come with forty links of chain. (Oh, Lordy)
Got my man and gone.

They tell me Joe Turner's come and gone.
They tell me Joe Turner's come and gone. (Oh, Lordy)
Done left me here to sing this song.

Come like he never come before.
Come like he never come before. (Oh, Lordy)
Got my man and gone.

Arrayed in stripes—the unmistakable badge of a convict—prisoners congregate in the yard of a southern jail.

"St. Louis Blues," the 1914 song by W. C. Handy, may be the best-known and most imitated blues ever written. Handy (1873–1958), the first composer to recognize the importance of the blues and to write them down, reveled in the song's fame. He was particularly pleased to hear that it had been featured in a command performance at "the palace"—Ethiopian emperor Haile Selassie's palace, that is—and he must have enjoyed this 1936 news story about the king of England:

Balmoral Castle, Scotland, Sept. 24—King Edward VIII ordered the nine pipers at Balmoral Castle to play "St. Louis Blues" today to entertain . . . guests on his vacation in Scotland, who were forced to spend most of the day indoors because of rain and high winds. The wind, adding to the wails of the Scottish bagpipes, made the "St. Louis Blues" really sound blue.

ST. LOUIS BLUES

By W. C. Handy

If the light from a night train falls through your barred window, says southern jailhouse legend, you will go free in the morning. In this bluesy song, inmates at the state prison farm in Sugar Land, Texas, listen to "The Midnight Special"—the California-bound "Sunset Limited" that roars out of Houston every night—and hear the sound of hope.

THE MIDNIGHT SPECIAL

Well, you wake up in the

morn - ing, ___ hear the big ___ bell ring, ___

You go march-ing to the ta - ble, ___ see the same damn' thing. ___

man. Let ___ the Mid-night Spe – cial ___ shine ___ her light on me, ___

Let ___ the Mid-night Spe – cial ___

shine her ev – er – lov – in' light on me. _____

If you ev – er go to ___

If you ever go to Houston, you'd better walk right,
And you better not stagger, and you better not fight.
'Cause the sheriff will arrest you and he'll carry you down,
And you can bet your bottom dollar you're Sugarland bound.
Chorus

Yonder comes Miss Rosie, tell me how do you know?
I know her by her apron and the dress she wore.
Umbrella on her shoulder, piece of paper in her hand,
Well, I heard her tell the captain, "I want my man."
Chorus

Lord, Thelma said she loved me, but I believe she told a lie,
'Cause she hasn't been to see me since last July.
She brought me little coffee, she brought me little tea.
She brought me nearly everything but the jail-house key.
Chorus

Well, the biscuits on the table, just as hard as any rock,
If you try to eat them, break a convict's heart.
My sister wrote a letter, my mother wrote a card—
"If you want to come to see us, you'll have to ride the rods."
Chorus

I'm goin' away to leave you, and my time it ain't long.
The man is gonna call me, and I'm goin' home.
Then I'll be done all my grievin', whoopin', hollerin', and a-cryin';
Then I'll be done all my studyin' 'bout my great long time.
Chorus

A westbound steam train roars out of a railroad station in the mid-1930s.

America, with its almost immeasurable sweeps of mountain, prairie, and seacoast, has always been a land of travelers. The frontier once seemed to stretch forever; if people did not like it where they were, why then, they could just move on. The nation's voices naturally followed its feet; wherever they gathered, Americans sang about the open road. Among the most popular "movin' on" ballads are: "Wanderin'," "I'm On My Way," "Brakeman's Blues," "Going Down the Road Feeling Bad," "Lonesome Road," and "Sixty-Six Highway Blues."

There is a road from the east to the west,
New York to Los Angeles.
I'm a-goin' down that road with worries on my mind,
I've got them Sixty-Six Highway Blues.

WANDERIN'

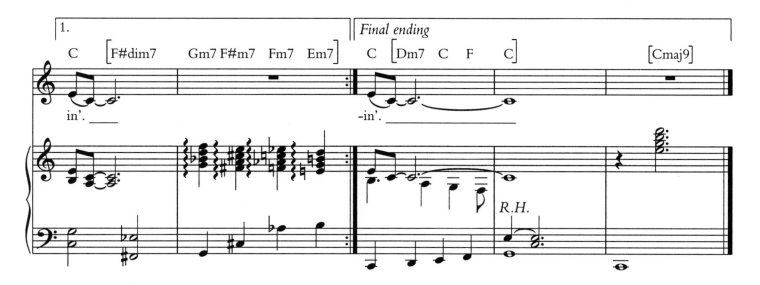

I've been a-wanderin' early and late,
New York City to the Golden Gate.
Chorus

Been a-workin' in the city; been a-workin' on the farm,
And all I've got to show for it is the muscle in my arm.
Chorus

Snakes in the ocean, eels in the sea,
A redheaded woman made a fool out of me.
Chorus

This is a companion piece to "The Midnight Special." Instead of being carried off to freedom on the express train's powerful beam, the prisoners are visited by their wives and sweethearts, who make a monthly trip from Houston to Sugar Land in a broken-down old car nicknamed Shorty George. The vehicle also carries the women away after the visit, leaving the men behind to sing the blues. ("Katy," in verse four, is a nickname for the Missouri, Kansas, and Texas railroad line.) In the 1930s, Shorty George took on a new meaning: it was the name of a jazz dance step that originated in the black community and became popular with young people of all races.

SHORTY GEORGE

Shorty George, he done been here and gone,
Yes, Shorty George, he done been here and gone,
Lord, he left many a poor man a great long way from home.

My mama died when I was a lad,
My mama died when I was a lad,
And ever since I been to the bad.

Well, my babe caught the Katy, I caught the Santa Fe(e),
Well, she caught the Katy and I caught the Santa Fe(e),
Well, you can't quit me, baby, can't you see?

Well, I went to Galveston – work on the Mallory Line,
Went to Galveston – Lord, on the Mallory Line,
Babe, you can't quit me – ain't no use tryin'.

Shorty George, travelin' through the land,
Shorty George, he's travelin' through the land,
Always lookin' to pick some poor woman's man.

When I get back to Dallas, I'm gonna walk and tell,
When I get back to Dallas, gonna walk and tell,
That the Fort Bend bottom is a burning hell.

Well-a, Shorty George, he ain't no friend of mine,
Well-a, Shorty George, he ain't no friend of mine,
He's taken all the women and left the men behind.

A prison blues often tells no "story"; it simply creates a mood, usually of loneliness and longing for the world outside the gate. The blues is "an especially effective medium for complaint, protest, and the venting of frustrations," points out music scholar Lawrence W. Levine, who adds that "these same qualities . . . make it difficult to interpret the meaning of many black songs." Whatever its meaning, "Been in the Pen So Long" is a powerful lament; it should be sung slowly and reflectively.

BEEN IN THE PEN SO LONG

Awful lonesome, all alone and blue,
Awful lonesome, all alone and blue.
All alone and blue,
No one to tell my troubles to,
Baby, where you been so long?
Baby, where you been so long?

Some folks crave for Memphis, Tennessee,
Some folks crave for Memphis, Tennessee,
Some folks crave
For Memphis, Tennessee,
But New Orleans is good enough for me,
New Orleans is good enough for me.

A convicted man seems to consider the empty years that lie ahead.

"Nobody gave us lessons," said the immortal Mississippi-born blues singer William "Big Bill" Broonzy (1893–1956), "it was just born in us to sing the blues." In this song, an inmate of Parchman, the notorious prison farm in southern Mississippi, begs his visiting girlfriend to remain: "It's cold down here," he laments. But he sorrowfully concedes that she has no choice: she must "go back to New Orleans," leaving him "way down here in a rollin' fog."

BABY, PLEASE DON'T GO

Words and Music by
William (Big Bill) Broonzy

Babe, I'm way down here,
You know, I'm way down here,
Babe, I'm way down here in a rollin' fog.
Baby, please don't go.

Baby, please don't go,
Baby, please don't go,
Baby, please don't go back to New Orleans,
You know, it hurts me so.

Babe, I'm way down here,
You know I'm way down here,
Babe, I'm way down here on old Parchman Farm,
Baby, please don't go.

Baby, please don't go,
Baby, please don't go,
Baby, please don't go and leave me here,
You know it's cold down here.

Babe, I'm way down here,
You know, I'm way down here,
Babe, I'm way down here on old Parchman Farm,
Baby, please don't go.

You know it's cold down here,
Babe, it's cold down here,
You know, it's cold down here on old Parchman Farm,
Baby, please don't go.

Baby, please don't go,
Baby, please don't go,
Baby, please don't go and leave me here,
You know it's cold down here.

I'm half dead down here,
I'm half dead down here,
I'm half dead down here on old Parchman Farm,
Baby, please don't go.

Referring both to a state of mind—the blues—and the state of the nation—America's economic collapse in the 1930s—the "Depression Blues" was written by Hudson Whittaker, a much admired slide guitar player known as Tampa Red. "A man like Tampa Red," said Big Bill Broonzy (in a 1955 interview with writer Yannick Bruynoghe), "has got a style of his own, playing guitar with a bottle neck on his little finger, sliding up and down the guitar strings." Tampa Red had many imitators, but none succeeded, asserted Broonzy, because "there is only one Tampa Red and when he's dead, that's all, brother."

DEPRESSION BLUES

By Tampa Red

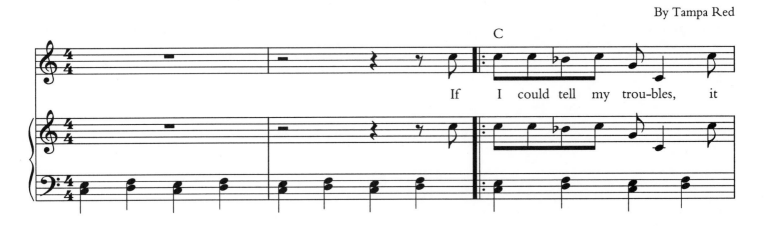

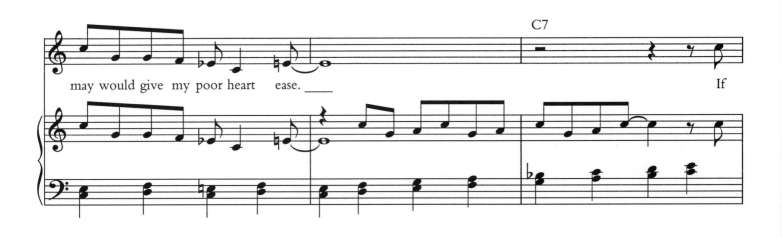

But de - pres - sions has got ___ me, some - bo - dy help me,

1.

please.

Final ending

If there. ___

If I don't feel no better than I feel today,
If I don't feel no better than I feel today,
I'm gonna pack my few clothes and make my getaway.

I've begged and I've borrowed till my friends don't want me 'round.
I've begged and I've borrowed till my friends don't want me 'round.
I'll take old man Depression and leave this no-good town.

Depression's here, they tell me it's everywhere;
Depression's here, they tell me it's everywhere;
So I'm going back to Florida and see if Depression's there.

Unemployed men line up outside a relief office in 1931, the peak year of the Great Depression.

BRICKS IN MY PILLOW

"Bricks in My Pillow" forms a sharp contrast to "Never No More Hard Times Blues." If there ever was a song to illustrate Murphy's Law—"if a thing can go wrong, it will"—this is it.

I've got bricks in my pil - low and my

head can't rest no—more. ___ I've got bricks _

___ in my pil - low and my head can't rest no— more. ___

I've got mud in my water, I've got drugs all in my tea.
I've got mud in my water, I've got drugs all in my tea.
I've got bugs in my beer, and they keep on biting me.

I've got grounds in my coffee, big boll weevil in my meal.
I've got grounds in my coffee, big boll weevil in my meal.
I've got tacks in my shoes, keep on stickin' me in the heel.

I've got holes in my pockets, great big patches on my pants.
I've got holes on my pockets, great big patches on my pants.
I'm behind with my house rent, landlord wants it in advance.

Well, I feel like walkin' and I feel like lyin' down.
Well, I feel like walkin' and I feel like lyin' down.
Well, I feel like drinkin', but there ain't no whisky 'round.

When you hear that bell ringin' and you hear that whistle blow.
When you hear that bell ringin' and you hear that whistle blow.
Well, I feel like leavin', but I don't know where to go.

This is a real rarity—an optimistic blues. In blues, as in most folk songs, good times are seldom the subject; people who are content with their lot, who have "made it," have left us almost no legacy in song. Instead, it has been the Tin Pan Alley songsmith who has given us the "Blue Skies" music. "Never No More Hard Times Blues" lies somewhere between the worlds of traditional realism and pop fantasy.

NEVER NO MORE HARD TIMES BLUES

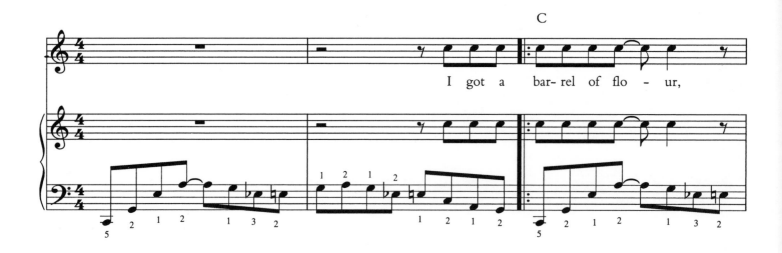

Got corn in my crib, got cotton in my patch.
Got corn in my crib, got cotton in my patch.
I got the old hen settin'— waitin' for the old hen to hatch.

I'm gonna build me a shanty, Lord, I'm gonna settle down.
I'm gonna build me a shanty, Lord, I'm gonna settle down.
Get me a cornfed mama, Lord, and stop runnin' around.

I can make more money with my pick and plow.
I can make more money with my pick and plow.
With my one-eyed mule and my good old Jersey cow.

Black folk music abounds with references to the boll weevil, a tiny but devastatingly destructive insect that could, and often did, wipe out the life's work of a southern farmer. The bug found its way from Mexico to Texas in the 1890s, and by the 1920s it had cut a swath of destruction through the South. In Greene Country, Georgia, for example, farmers produced more than 20,000 bales of cotton in 1919; in 1922, the harvest was 333 bales. Despite the weevil's devilishness, most black songs about him have an admiring tone—as though blacks could do little but respect a creature who, like themselves, stood up to everything the enemy could do to him. "Boll Weevil Blues" is typical of the many wry tributes to this indomitable creature.

BOLL WEEVIL BLUES

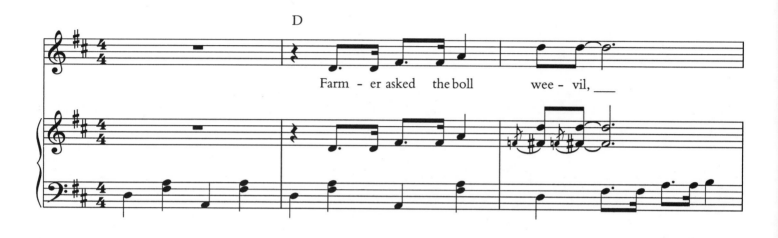

Farm - er asked the boll wee - vil, ___

"Where you been—so long?" ___ "I been down in the

cot - ton, ___ With my long clothes on."

Farmer take the boll weevil,
Put him in the ice.
Boll weevil say to the farmer,
"You treat me mighty nice."

Farmer take the boll weevil,
He put him in the sand.
Boll weevil say to the farmer,
"You just like a man."

Man said to the old lady,
"What do you think of that?
I got one of them boll weevils
Out of my Stetson hat."

Farmer said to the boll weevil,
"Yes, I wish you well."
He said to the boll weevil,
"I hope you burn in hell."

Boll weevil said to the farmer,
"I'm gonna swing on your gate,
When I get through with your cotton,
You'll sell your Cadillac eight."

Boll weevil said to the farmer,
"I'm gonna treat you mean,
When I get through with your cotton,
You buy no gasoline."

Farm workers harvest cotton on a Mississippi plantation.

After Big Bill Broonzy wrote this song in 1945, he found no one willing to record it. He talked about it with his biographer, Yannick Bruynoghe, in 1955. When the record companies said that people would not buy such a song, recalled Broonzy, he had responded:

> What's wrong with it? I would like to know. What I say is just about the way the working Negro is treated in this country on all the jobs in the South, in the North, in the East and in the West, and you all know it's true.

> "Yes," they would say to me, "and that is what's wrong with this song. You see, Bill, when you write a song and want to record it with any company, it must keep the people guessing what the song means. Don't you say what it means when you're singing. And that song comes right to the point and the public won't like that."

As things turned out, the song *was* recorded. Its 1951 release (on the Vogue label) was greeted with great enthusiasm by Broonzy fans both in the United States and France, where black American folk music was enjoying a wave of popularity.

BLACK, BROWN, AND WHITE BLUES

Words and Music by
William (Big Bill) Broonzy

I was in a place one night,
They was all having fun,
They was all drinking beer and wine,
But me, I couldn't buy none.
    Chorus

I was in an employment office,
Got a number and fell in line,
They called every number,
But they never did call mine.
    Chorus

Me and a man working side by side,
This is what it meant:
He was getting a dollar an hour,
I was only making fifty cents.
    Chorus

I helped build this country,
I fought for it too;
Now I guess that you can see
What a black man has got to do.
    Chorus

I helped to win this vict'ry
With my spade and hoe,
Now I wanna know—
Whatcha gonna do about the Jim Crow?
    Chorus

A family of field hands takes a midday break on an Arkansas farm.

During the dark days of slavery, southern blacks looked toward the North as the Promised Land: "Follow the Drinking Gourd," they sang, referring to the Big Dipper and its north-pointing handle. Years after the Civil War, the North continued to exert a magnetic pull on southern blacks; to the impoverished farm workers of Mississippi and Alabama, stories of the industrialized North with its humming factories, thousands of jobs, and "good money" offered an irresistible vision of prosperity. "Michigan Water Blues" expressed just such an image, although the reality was usually closer to Broonzy's picture in "Black, Brown and White Blues."

MICHIGAN WATER BLUES

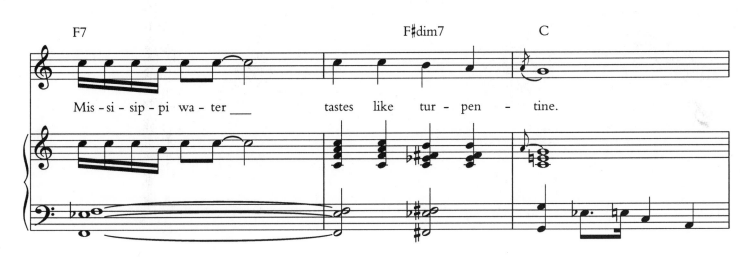

I   I believe to my soul I've got to leave this place,
     Goin' away where the folks don't know my face.
     Michigan water tastes like sherry wine.

II   Gal in Lou'siana — one in Maine,
     Got one in Mississippi, scared to call her name.
     Michigan water tastes like sherry wine,
     Michigan water tastes like sherry wine.

Former slaves gather for a portrait with Harriet Tubman (far left), the Underground Railroad "conductor" who led them to freedom.

The train occupies a unique place in the folk songs of black and white Americans alike. When the steel rails began crossing the continent in the 19th century, they revolutionized the way people thought about the land: it was now possible to travel from one distant point to another in hours or days instead of weeks or months. Songs about building the railroads, traveling on the railroads, robbing the railroads, even dying on the railroads, became standard fare. For some reason, the "two-nineteen" is often the train of choice, figuring in a number of blues and ballads.

TWO-NINETEEN BLUES

Two-nine-teen __ took my babe a-way,

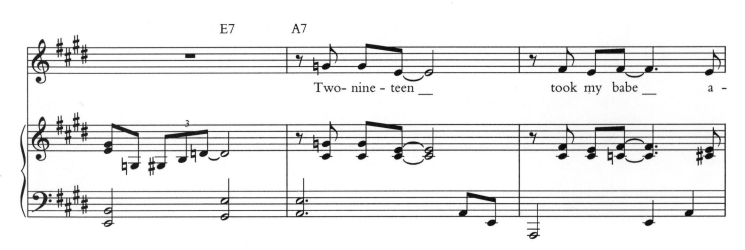

Two-nine-teen __ took my babe __ a-

Stood on the corner with her feet soakin' wet,
Stood on the corner with her feet soakin' wet,
Beggin' each and every man that she met.

If you can't give a dollar give me a lousy dime,
If you can't give a dollar give me a lousy dime,
I want to feed that hungry man of mine.

Blind Lemon Jefferson (c. 1897–c. 1930) was a rough, authentic folk singer and guitar player from Couchman, Texas. He earned his living by performing on the streets of Texas towns, often with Leadbelly (immortal folk singer Huddie Ledbetter; 1885–1949). Jefferson's "voice was high, piercing the traffic noise," note the authors of *Gospel, Blues and Jazz* (W. W. Norton, 1986), "but it could also have a low, moaning quality extended by 'bending' the notes on his guitar to produce crying sounds." Jefferson developed a strong following in the Southwest.

At the same time, phonograph records were becoming increasingly popular. Recognizing a profitable market in the black community, several companies introduced what they called "race records"—music made by and for blacks. "The World's Greatest Race Artists on the World's Greatest Race Records," boasted Okeh Records; the black-owned Black Swan label advertised its product as "The Only Genuine Colored Record. All Others Are Only Passing for Colored." Responding to demands by consumers, a small Chicago mail-order record company, Paramount ("The Popular Race Record"), brought the 29-year-old Jefferson to Chicago, where he recorded eight songs, all released in 1926 and all immediate best-sellers among midwestern and southern blacks. One of these songs was "Lonesome House Blues," which, along with the classic "Match Box Blues" and "One Dime Blues," is among Jefferson's finest compositions. After his untimely death—the blind musician was found frozen to death in a Chicago snowbank at the age of 33—dozens of other singers recorded his powerful blues songs.

LONESOME HOUSE BLUES

I'm goin' away, momma, just to wear you off my mind.
I'm goin' away, pretty momma, just to wear you off my mind.
If I live here in Chicago, money's gonna be my crime.

My house is lonesome, my baby left me all alone.
This house is lonesome — she left me all alone.
If your heart ain't rock, sugar, it must be marble stone.

I got the blues so bad, it hurts my feet to walk.
I got the blues so bad, it hurts my feet to walk.
It has settled on my brain, and it hurts my tongue to talk.

The "Rider"—sometimes "Easy Rider," sometimes "C. C." or "See See Rider"—is a legendary sweet-talking man who blows into town and immediately finds a woman who will love and support him until he moves on. He often packs a guitar (which always helps), and sometimes turns out to be a hustler. The "Rider" character has inspired dozens of songs; here is one of the best.

C. C. RIDER

now _____ your wo-man's come.   You

You caused me, Rider, to hang my head and cry,
You put me down; God knows I don't see why.
You put me down; God knows I don't see why.
You put me down; God knows I don't see why.

If I had a headlight like on a passenger train,
I'd shine my light on cool Colorado Springs.
I'd shine my light on cool Colorado Springs.
I'd shine my light on cool Colorado Springs.

That Sunshine Special comin' 'round the bend,
It blowed just like it never blowed before.
It blowed just like it never blowed before.
It blowed just like it never blowed before.

A dashing young man-about-town escorts two women to Harlem's exclusive Negro Ball in the 1940s.

The image of a great iron machine whistling through the night sky and carrying loved ones away forever is the stuff from which blues are made. Central to the train's appeal is its mournful whistle, which blues guitarists and other musicians can imitate to perfection. Blues harmonica players evoke the train's desolate voice with breath control and by cupping their hands or fluttering their fingers over their instruments. Some go further, alternating their own voices with that of the harmonica to create an ongoing flow of music.

NUMBER 12 TRAIN

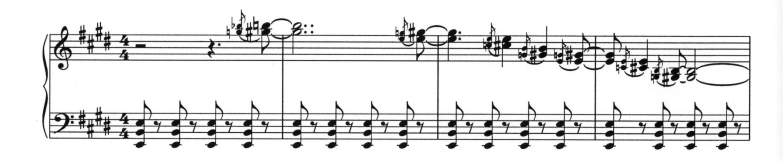

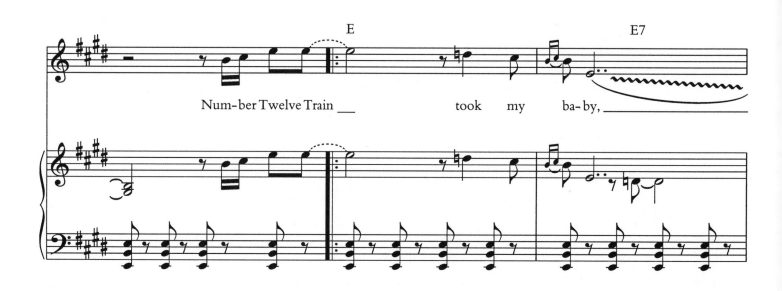

Num-ber Twelve Train ___ took my ba-by, ___

___ I could not keep from cry'n'. ___   Num-ber

She left me all night long, I could not help myself.
She left me all night long, I could not help myself.
I thought she was lovin' me — I found she had someone else.

I may be wrong, but I'll be right some day;
I may be wrong, but I'll be right some day;
'Cause the next gal I get will have to do what Poppa say.

An important characteristic of the blues is its urge to define and explain itself; just think of the enormous number of blues songs with the word *blues* in their titles.

The phrase "ain't nothin' but . . ." often pops up in the blues: "The blues ain't nothin' but a poor man's heart disease," "Them blues ain't nothin' but a woman lost her man," or "Love ain't nothin' but the blues," for example.

THE BLUES AIN'T NOTHIN'

I'm gon-na build my-self a raft _____ And float that ri-ver

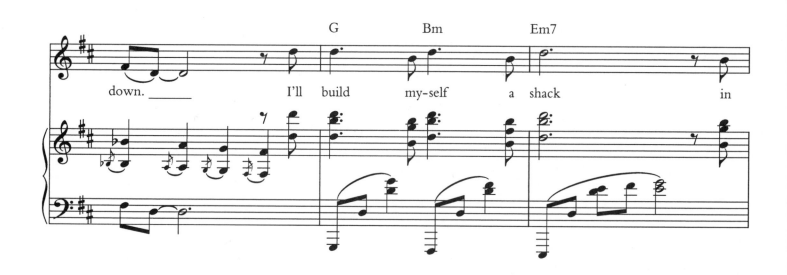

down. _____ I'll build my-self a shack in

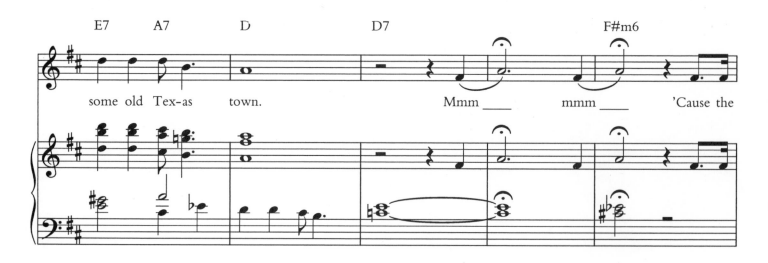

some old Tex-as town. Mmm ___ mmm ___ 'Cause the

blues ain't noth-in', No, the blues ain't noth-in' but a

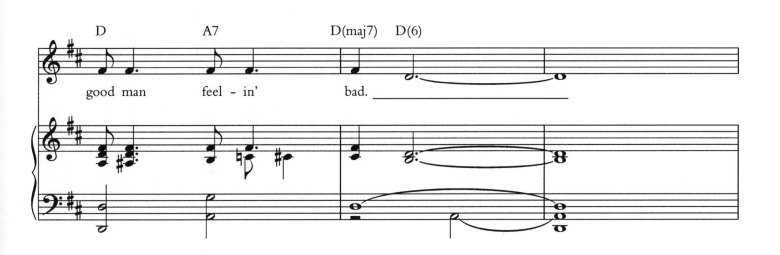

good man feel-in' bad. _____

I'm goin' down on the levee,
Goin' to take myself a rockin' chair.
If my lovin' gal don't come,
I'll rock away from there.
Mmm—mmm . . .
'Cause the blues ain't nothin',
No, the blues ain't nothin'
But a good man feelin' bad.

Why did you leave me blue?
Why did you leave me blue?
All I can do is sit
And cry and cry for you.
Mmm—mmm . . .
'Cause the blues ain't nothin',
No, the blues ain't nothin'
But a good man feelin' bad.

The sentiments expressed in the second verse of "Lonesome Blues" echo those of the Elizabethan troubadour who, four centuries ago, sang these words:

And if you meet a lady gay
As you go by the hill, sir,
If you will not when you may,
You shall not when you will, sir.

Perhaps this proves, once again, that there is nothing new under the sun—at least in matters of the heart.

LONESOME BLUES

I may be down and out to-day, but I'll be up some-day.

Boys, ain't it hard lovin' another man's girl friend?
Can't see her when you want to, got to see her when you can.
   Chorus

I got to walk by myself, sleep by myself,
While the woman I love she's lovin' somebody else.
   Chorus

My baby left me, she left me broken down,
Said, "Goodbye, daddy, I'll meet you in another town."
   Chorus

I wake up in the morning, 'bout the break of day,
Reach against the pillow where my baby used to lay.
   Chorus

This song's internal refrain—an unusual feature in a blues—reveals its work-song roots and, at the same time, conceals a double meaning. Sweets often serve as "thinly veiled sexual metaphors," notes scholar Lawrence W. Levine. "When black songs depict men stealing, cheating, and dying for jelly roll, angel food cake, or shortening bread, it is difficult to believe that these terms refer to food," he adds. "Shuckin' Sugar Blues" was among the many suggestive songs that helped make Blind Lemon Jefferson a recording success in the 1920s.

SHUCKIN' SUGAR BLUES

I've got your pic-ture, _____ and I'm goin' to put it in a frame; ___

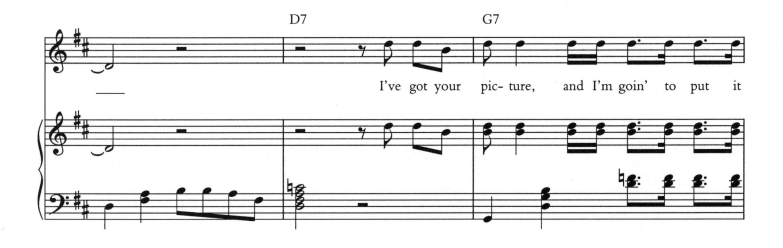

___ I've got your pic-ture, and I'm goin' to put it

in a frame—Shuck-in' sug-ar ___ And then if

you leave town we can find you just the same. _____

Now, if you don't love me, please don't dog me 'round.
If you don't love me, please don't dog me 'round
— Shuckin' sugar—
If you dog me 'round I know you'll put me down.

Oh, say, Sarah Brown, somethin's gone on wrong.
Say, Sarah Brown, somethin's done gone wrong
— Shuckin' sugar—
The woman I love, she done been here and gone.

Oh, listen Sarah Brown, don't you want to go?
Oh, Sarah Brown, don't you want to go?
— Shuckin' sugar—
Want to take you 'cross the water where that
    brown-skin man can't go.

I am worried here, and I'm worried everywhere.
I am worried here, and I'm worried everywhere
— Shuckin' sugar—
Man, I stretched out at home, and I'll not be worried there.

I'm tired of marryin', tired of this settlin' down.
Tired of bein' married, tired of this settlin' down
— Shuckin' sugar—
I only want to stay like I am and slip from town to town.

Keeping a wary eye on each other, a trio of well-dressed Chicagoans share a booth at the neighborhood tavern.

Folk music abounds with star-crossed sweethearts, men and women crazy in love who end up destroying each other. The best known of these doomed pairs is probably Frankie and Johnny (sometimes called Frankie and Albert). Frankie winds up on the gallows for blowing away the unfaithful Johnny:

First time she shot him, he staggered,
Next time she shot him, he fell,
Third time she shot him O Lawdy,
There was a new man's face in hell.
She killed her man,
For doing her wrong.

The love affair of Betty and Dupree also ends in tragedy. Like Railroad Bill, Stagolee, and John Hardy, Dupree is one of black folklore's larger-than-life "bad men," but at least he tries to do right by his Betty. Nevertheless, when he is trying to steal the diamond ring she has asked for, he kills a policeman and winds up at the end of a rope.

BETTY AND DUPREE

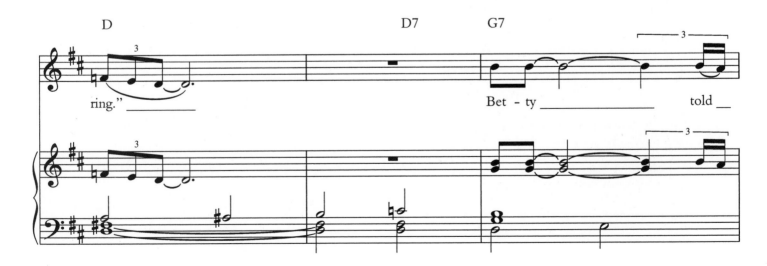

He said, "Lie down, little Betty, see what to-
    morrow brings,"
He said, "Lie down, little Betty, see what to-
    morrow brings."
"It may bring sunshine, may bring you that
    diamond ring."

Then he got his pistol, went to the jewelry
    store.
He got his pistol, went to the jewelry store.
Killed a policeman and he wounded four or
    five more.

Then he went to the post office to get his eve-
    ning mail, oh, babe.
Went to the post office to get his evening mail.
Sheriff caught poor Dupree and put him in that
    old Atlanta jail.

Dupree's mother said to Betty, "Looka here
    what you done done."
She said to Betty, "See what you done done,"
    oh, babe.
"Made my boy rob and steal, now he is gonna
    be hung."

"Give my daddy my clothes — poor Betty, give
    her my shoes," oh, babe.
"Give my daddy my clothes, give my baby,
    Betty, my shoes.
"If anybody asks you, say I died with the heart-
    breaking blues."

Sail on, sail on, sail on, Dupree, sail on.
Sail on, sail on, sail on, Dupree, sail on.
You don't mind sailing, you'll be gone so dog-
    gone long.

The singer here is not only "broke and hungry, ragged and dirty too," but bemoaning the loss of all he had: parents, siblings, sweetheart, even his magical "black cat bone." This is the *blues*.

BROKE AND HUNGRY BLUES

I _____ am broke and hun- gry, rag - g'd and dir - ty too. _

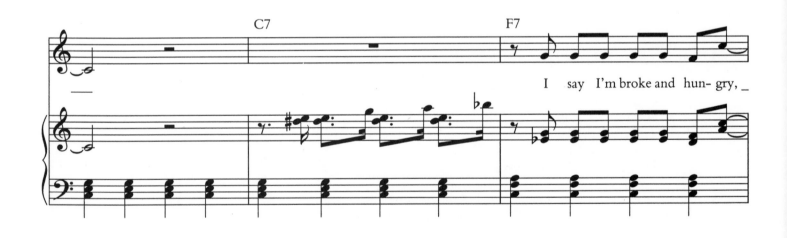

I say I'm broke and hun- gry, _

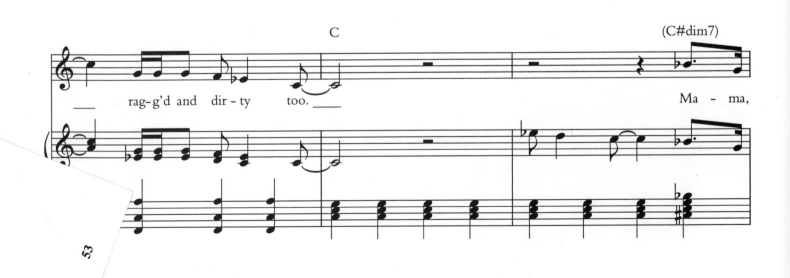

_ rag-g'd and dir - ty too. _____ Ma - ma,

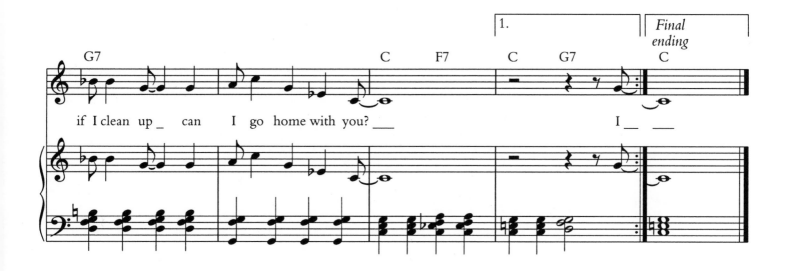

if I clean up _ can I go home with you? ___ I _ ___

I am motherless, fatherless, sister- and brotherless too.
I say I'm motherless, fatherless, sister- and brotherless too.
Reason I tried so hard to make this trip with you.

You miss me, woman, count the days I'm gone.
You miss me, woman, count the days I'm gone.
I'm goin' away to build me a railroad of my own.

I feel like jumpin' through the keyhole in your door.
I feel like jumpin' through the keyhole in your door.
If you jump this time, baby, you won't jump no more.

I believe my good gal has found my black cat bone.
I say, I b'lieve my good gal has found my black cat bone.
I can leave Sunday morning; Monday morning I'm stickin' 'round home.

I want to show you women what careless love has done.
I want to show you women what careless love has done.
Cause a man like me to be 'way, 'way from home.

When federal price controls ended after World War II, inflation skyrocketed in America. This song was born during that era, but its message of protest could apply to any period when times are hard for the poor. Most prominently connected with "High Price Blues" are guitarist Brownie McGhee and blind harmonica player Sonny Terry, musicians whose close partnership impressed blues fans and musicologists for 35 years. "Terry's crying harmonica and guttural, sometimes slightly off-key vocals," note the authors of *Gospel, Blues and Jazz*, "were offset by McGhee's light, smooth guitar playing and mellow singing."

HIGH PRICE BLUES

I'll tell you some-thing, ain't no joke,

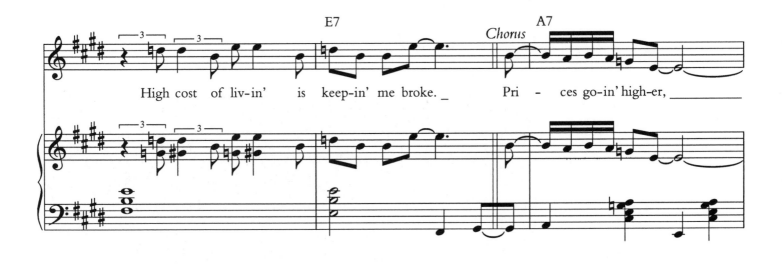

High cost of liv-in' is keep-in' me broke. ___ Pri — ces go-in' high-er, _____

___ 'way ___ up high-er, ___ Pri-ces go-in' so high, _____ what

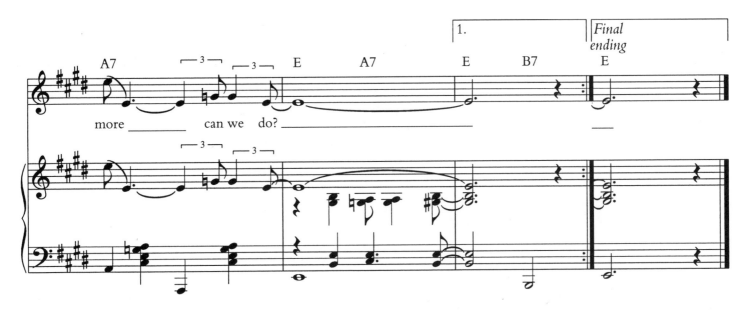

Walked in a meat market just about noon,
Hear them hollerin', "Now the cow jumped over the moon."
Chorus

Johnny's gone to war, Jimmy's gone to sea,
But I tell you high prices is killin' me.
Chorus

Meat, butter, and eggs gettin' higher still,
You don't even get no change out of a five-dollar bill.
Chorus:
Prices goin' higher; yes, 'way up higher,
Well, it's no disgrace to be poor, but it's a little unhandy for me.

The horses and the numbers — odds are still the same,
Looks like the prices would raise ten per cent on the game.
Chorus:
Prices goin' higher; yes, 'way up higher.
Prices goin' so high, I don't think I will work no more.

A farm woman painstakingly counts out her money at an eastern Missouri grocery store in 1930, the second year of the Great Depression.

World War II, which the United States entered in 1941, began to produce changes in the status of black men in America. The government limited black soldiers to "Negro units," but—in a major departure from World War I—it trained many for combat. All-black divisions fought side by side with all-white divisions, allowing the black soldiers to prove their extraordinary courage as fighting men. World War II also saw the establishment of an all-black fighter squadron, the celebrated 332nd Fighter Group, led by black flying ace general Benjamin O. Davis. But progress or not, nobody enjoyed being a draftee, and black and white recruits bewailed their lot with equal vigor. "Draftee's Blues" takes a seriocomic look at the situation.

DRAFTEE'S BLUES

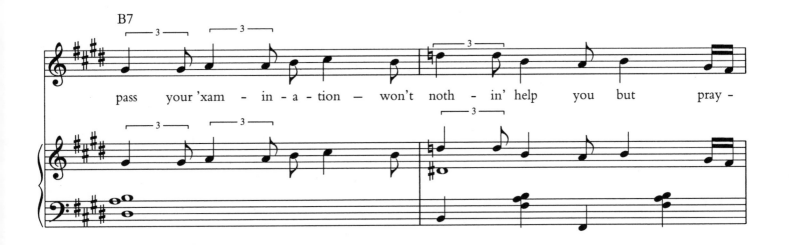

pass your 'xam - in - a - tion — won't noth - in' help you but pray -

er. _____ They will ___

They will take you to the depot and put you on the train,
Yes, they'll take you to the depot— put you on the train,
And the Good Lord only knows if you'll be comin' home again.

There's no need to worry—hatin' to leave your happy home,
There's no need to worry—hatin' to leave your happy home,
Because there'll be someone left behind to carry all your lovin' on.

You may be mean as a lion, you may be gentle as a lamb,
You may be mean as a lion— gentle as a lamb,
Just take your mind off your wife and put it on Uncle Sam.

They will train you with a rifle—Lord, with a hand grenade,
They will train you with a rifle—Lord, with a hand grenade,
So when you meet that Nazi, man, you won't be afraid.

I want all of you draftees to put your mind on your training camp,
I want all of you draftees to put your mind on your training camp,
So when you meet old Hitler your powder won't be damp.

I want to tell you women just as easy as I can,
I want to tell all you women— easy as I can,
Uncle Sam ain't no woman but he sure can take your man.

Although the overwhelming majority of the 404,000 blacks who served America in World War I (1917–18) were assigned to service units, those who did see action fought gallantly. In fact, no regiment, black or white, earned more wartime glory than the "Hell Fighters"—the 369th Infantry Regiment of the 93rd Infantry Division. This all-black unit, in continuous combat longer than any other American military group, was the first Allied regiment to reach the crucial Rhine River in the offensive against Germany. The *I* in "When I Lay Down" is a black American soldier fighting in France; when he mentions "ten thousand plunkers," he is referring to the $10,000 life insurance policy the government wrote for each American soldier serving in European combat.

WHEN I LAY DOWN

When I lay down ___ and die on my old tired hun - kers, the

fam - 'ly back home - 'll get ten thou - sand plun - kers; Oh, ___

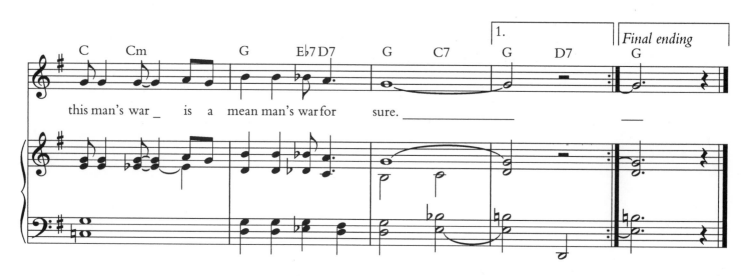

this man's war _ is a mean man's war for sure. _____

I only want to live but I know I've got to die,
The fun I'll have be in the sweet by and by;
Oh, this man's war is a mean man's war for sure.

All of those mamas back home are a-pinin'
For a papa like me when the moon is a-shinin';
Oh, this man's war is a mean man's war for sure.

Can't think about livin' when you know you got to die,
Can't think about lovin' when the heinie's nearby;
Oh, this man's war is a mean man's war for sure.

Findin' out every day how to be a fighter,
I'm a-totin' my gun but my pack's gettin' lighter;
Oh, this man's war is a mean man's war for sure.

There's a sniper over yonder in what's left of a tree,
But he'll be a snipin' son of gun before he ever snipes me;
Oh, this man's war is a mean man's war for sure.

A World War II bomber crew prepares for an air strike over Italy.

The lament of the young woman gone wrong, led astray by a bad man and now unable to rise above her fate, appears in literature and folklore all over the world, but rarely does it appear as directly as in black American music, the blues in particular. In 1890, black Texas workers sang:

> *Well, Baby, your house rent's due, Baby, your house rent's due;*
> *Just put on your bustle and make a little rustle,*
> *And bring in a dollar or two.*

Mississippi-born Charley Patton (c. 1887–1934), one of America's most celebrated bluesmen, sang of the same subject, notably in "Moon Going Down," which he recorded in 1930. After complaining that his woman has left him, he sings of the prostitutes who will comfort him: "There's a house over yonder painted all over green. . . . Some of the finest young women, Lord, man most ever seen."

"House of the Rising Sun," a classic musical treatment of prostitution, was one of the trademarks of the legendary singer-guitarist Josh White (1915–69), who recorded it for ground-breaking jazz producer Creed Taylor in 1957.

THE HOUSE OF THE RISING SUN

girl, and me, oh, Lord, _ was _ one. _____ If ___

If I had listened what Mama said, I'd 'a' been at home today,
Being so young and foolish, poor boy, let a gambler lead me astray.

My mother, she's a tailor, she sold those new blue jeans;
My sweetheart, he's a drunkard, Lord, drinks down in New Orleans.

The only thing a drunkard needs is a suitcase and a trunk,
The only time he's satisfied is when he's on a drunk.

Go tell my baby sister never do like I have done,
To shun that house in New Orleans they call the Rising Sun.

One foot is on the platform and the other one on the train,
I'm going back to New Orleans to wear that ball and chain.

I'm going back to New Orleans, my race is almost run,
Going back to spend the rest of my life beneath that Rising Sun.

Fashionably dressed—but showing a bit too much leg for a "lady" of 1910—a young prostitute sits for a photographer in New Orleans.

Index to Titles

Index to first lines

Jerry Silverman is one of America's most prolific authors of music books. He has a B.S. degree in music from the City College of New York and an M.A. in musicology from New York University. He has authored some 100 books dealing with various aspects of guitar, banjo, violin, and fiddle technique, as well as numerous songbooks and arrangements for other instruments. He teaches guitar and music to children and adults and performs in folk-song concerts before audiences of all ages.

Kenneth B. Clark received a Ph.D. in social psychology from Columbia University and is the author of numerous books and articles on race and education. His books include *Prejudice and Your Child*, *Dark Ghetto*, and *Pathos of Power*. Long noted as an authority on segregation in schools, his work was cited by the U.S. Supreme Court in its decision in the historic *Brown v. Board of Education of Topeka* case in 1954. Dr. Clark, Distinguished Professor of Psychology Emeritus at the City University of New York, is the president of Kenneth B. Clark & Associates, a consulting firm specializing in personnel matters, race relations, and affirmative action programs.